cloverleaf books™

Holidays and Special Days

Brandon's Birthday Surprise

Lisa Bullard

illustrated by Katie Saunders

M MILLBROOK PRESS · MINNEAPOLIS

For Matt —L.B.
To my children Archie Gray
and Olive Honey —K.S.

Millbrook Press
A division of Lerner Publishing Group, Inc.
241 First Avenue North
Minneapolis, MN 55401 U.S.A.

Website address: www.lernerbooks.com

Main body text set in Slappy Inline 18/28.
Typeface provided by T26.

Library of Congress Cataloging-in-Publication Data

Bullard, Lisa.
    Brandon's birthday surprise / by Lisa Bullard ; illustrated by
Katie Saunders.
        p.   cm. — (Cloverleaf books. Holidays and special days)
    Includes index.
    ISBN 978-0-7613-5085-9 (lib. bdg. : alk. paper)
    1. Birthdays—Juvenile literature. I. Saunders, Katie ill.
II. Title.
GT2430.B85 2012
394.2—dc23   2011021514

Manufactured in the United States of America
1 – BP – 12/31/11

TABLE OF CONTENTS

Chapter One

A Special Birthday

Hi, I'm Brandon. This is my big brother, Riley. Can you keep a secret?

We're planning a **surprise** birthday party.

Somebody special was **born** on this **date!**

Today our **mom** turns **one year older.** She's out shopping right now. We're going to surprise her when she gets home!

PARTYLAND

FLOUR

People have not always celebrated birthdays. Birthday parties began in the last two hundred years or so. Before then, people mostly kept track of when leaders such as kings, queens, or presidents were born.

Chapter Two

Planning the Party

Riley and I want to show Mom just how special she is.

Some people's birthdays have become holidays. Martin Luther King Jr. was a great African American leader. His birthday is a U.S. holiday. We celebrate Martin Luther King Jr. Day on the third Monday of each January.

We bake a huge **birthday cake.** Then we make it look **super fancy!**

We put candles on the cake too. There's one for every year of Mom's life.

Many people make a wish before they blow out their candles. They try to blow them out with one big breath. If they do, they believe their wish will come true.

PARTYLAND

Look at all of them! I'll probably have to help her blow them out.

CANDLES

Riley is painting Mom a picture for her **present**.
I'm making her **birthday card**.

I'll add glitter to make it shine!

13

Chapter Three

Birthdays around the World

Our neighbor Sofia just stopped by! Sofia's family lived in Mexico before they moved to the United States.

Sofia is helping us make a **piñata**. She says piñatas are popular at **birthdays in Mexico.**

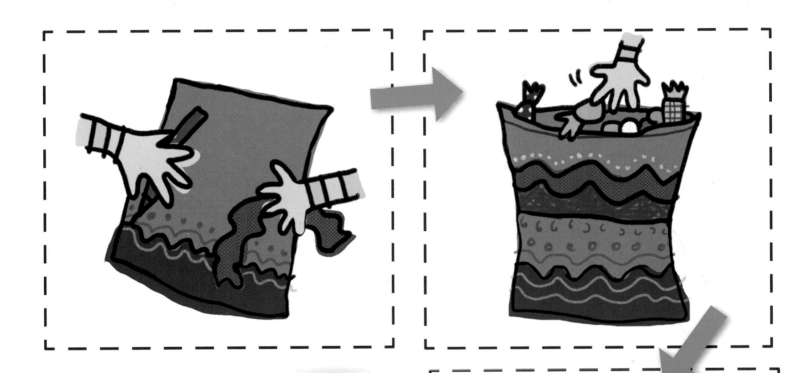

A piñata has candy and toys inside. A piñata hangs from a string. People take turns swinging at it with sticks. The person swinging wears a blindfold. Treats fall out after the piñata breaks open.

Mom should be home soon. We **practice** singing "Happy Birthday to You," extra loud.

Our dog, Lucy, sings along.

CANDY

16

People sing "Happy Birthday to You" all around the world. The song's words have been translated into many different languages. It has even been sung in outer space!

PARTYLAND

Everything's ready. We just need to hide.
But first, we try some of the extra piñata
candy. We want to make sure it tastes
good enough for Mom.

Other countries also have special birthday foods. Many people in China eat long noodles on their birthdays. Children in Australia eat fairy bread. Fairy bread is white bread with butter spread on top. People sprinkle colored sugar on the bread.

Chapter Four

Surprise!

Mom is home! We jump out of our hiding places when she walks in. We all yell, **"Happy birthday!"**

CANDY

Look at her face. We sure did surprise her!

Make an Easy Piñata

Some piñatas are very big or fancy. People often buy fancy piñatas at the store. But you can make your own easy piñata. You probably already have most of the things you need.

Equipment:

a paper bag (a grocery bag for a big piñata or a lunch bag for a smaller piñata)

wrapped candy, fruit snacks, stickers, or small toys

a piece of string, about 6 feet (2 meters) long

newspaper, balled up (optional)

colored tissue paper, streamers, or ribbons, cut or torn into 12-inch-long (30-centimeter) strips

stapler

hole punch

markers

glue

scissors

plastic baseball bat

a clean dish towel or handkerchief (to be used as a blindfold)

1) Decorate the bag. Glue colored streamers, tissue paper, or ribbons onto your piñata at one end. Then they will swirl when the piñata moves. You can also glue other paper cutouts onto your piñata or color it with markers. Let the glue dry for 1 hour or more.

2) Fill your piñata with the treats and toys until it is about halfway full. If you want a very round piñata, you can also add balled-up newspaper. Pack the paper in loosely until the bag is almost full.

3) Fold down the top of the bag twice. Then staple down the fold in three or four places. Use the hole punch to make two holes into the folded part, about 3 inches (8 cm) apart. Run the string through the two holes. Tie the ends of the string together.

4) Ask a grown-up to hang up your piñata using the string. The piñata should hang in an open area where you can safely swing the bat.

5) Invite your friends over. Take turns putting on the blindfold and swinging the bat. When someone breaks the piñata, share the treats and the toys!

GLOSSARY

blindfold: something tied over someone's eyes so they can't see

celebrate: to do something special to show that a day is important

fancy: extra special or with lots of decorations

favorite: the one you like the most

piñata (pin-YAH-tuh): a decorated container filled with toys and candy, used as a game at birthdays in countries such as Mexico

popular: something that is very well-liked

BOOKS

Brown, Marc. _Arthur's Birthday Surprise._ New York: Little, Brown, 2004.
Follow along as Arthur saves the day on his sister D.W.'s birthday.

Marzollo, Jean. _Happy Birthday, Martin Luther King._ New York: Scholastic, 2006.
This book explains why we celebrate the birthday of Martin Luther King Jr.

WEBSITES

Birthdays around the World
http://www.childrensmuseum.org/special_exhibits/worldwidebirthday/birthday_world.html
Check out this website from the Children's Museum of Indianapolis to learn more about birthdays around the world or events from your birth year. You can also hear birthday songs in different languages.

Enchanted Kitchen: Butterfly Fairy Bread
http://www.enchantedkitchen.net/2009/01/little-chefs.html
This easy-to-follow recipe will help you celebrate your next birthday with a slice of fairy bread.

PBS Kids Go!: Maya's Card Creator
http://pbskids.org/mayaandmiguel/english/games/cardcreator/index.html
Make a birthday card with this website's fun card creator. Then you can print it out or e-mail it to someone special.

LERNER **e** SOURCE™

Expand learning beyond the printed book. Download free, complementary educational resources for this book from our website, www.lernersource.com.